OLD WESTBURY GARDENS

Book
OF
Days

RIZZOLI
NEW YORK

Old Westbury Gardens Book of Days

To Honor

PEGGIE PHIPPS BOEGNER

First published in the United States of America in 1993 by
Rizzoli International Publications, Inc.
300 Park Avenue South, New York, New York 10010 and
Old Westbury Gardens, Box 430, Old Westbury, New York 11568

Text by Joyce Christmas, with Laura Carpenter

Copyright © 1993 Old Westbury Gardens

Front Cover illustration: The central pavilion of the Walled Garden
pergola and Lotus Pool. *Photo: Richard Cheek*

Designed by Christina Bliss

Printed in Singapore

Still, our main objective has been to preserve the charm and beauty of the Gardens in the tradition of my parents during their long and happy years and to offer a sense of delight and beauty to the gentle, welcome visitors.

—PEGGIE PHIPPS BOEGNER

Old Westbury Gardens, located on 160 acres of Long Island's North Shore, was formed in 1959 to preserve and protect for the public the estate of John S. ("Jay") and Margarita ("Dita") Grace Phipps.

The Charles II style house was begun in 1904 under the guidance of Jay Phipps, designer George Crawley, and architect Grosvenor Atterbury. Crawley was also instrumental, with Margarita Phipps, in the creation of the formal gardens and landscaped parks and woodlands of the estate.

Old Westbury Gardens is listed on the National Register of Historic Places by the United States Department of the Interior. The Gardens attract annually some 80,000 visitors who share in its program of lectures, concerts, exhibitions, tours, and seminars, and who enjoy the beauty of the Gardens and the splendor of Westbury House, which exists today as it did during the lifetime of Jay and Margarita Phipps.

Old Westbury Gardens would like to thank Fiat USA and Ferrari NA for their generous sponsorship of this publication.

*T*he *Old Westbury Gardens Book of Days* is fittingly dedicated to Peggie Phipps Boegner, who has called Old Westbury home throughout her life. No one has labored more diligently and lovingly to preserve the unique treasure that is Westbury House and its Gardens as they were established by her parents, John S. and Margarita Grace Phipps.

This lovely book captures the parade of the seasons, the changing weather, and the hours of the day at Old Westbury Gardens as Peggie knew them as a child and as she continues to enjoy them today.

For decades, the Gardens have unfailingly burst into bloom in the summer, slipped softly into the colors of autumn, and rested under the snows of winter, only to bloom anew with the coming of spring. In the Gardens today, new plant varieties are mixed with the old to surprise our visitors with a delightful freshness.

As we turn these pages, marking the rounds of our busy days, we can glimpse again a moment in full summer in the Italianate Walled Garden, dedicated to the memory of Margarita Phipps; the great trees rising out of the mysterious mists of early morning; the sun falling on the brilliant autumn leaves of the sugar maples; and the snow-bedecked topiaries guarding the South Lawn of Westbury House.

We are refreshed and inspired by these remarkable views of the formal gardens, lawns, allées, and woodlands of Old Westbury Gardens. They are a constant reminder that, however much the world around us changes, there remains an enduring sanctuary for us, full of natural beauty.

Old Westbury Gardens has many friends who are committed to preserving the memory of a vanished era in our cultural and social history. Like Peggie Phipps Boegner, they strive to maintain the Gardens as a serene oasis where thousands of visitors each year find peace and a renewal of the spirit. And like Peggie, they are certain that their efforts are making it possible to pass on this heritage of beauty to future generations.

Mary Phipps
President
Old Westbury Gardens

J A N U A R Y

1

2

3

4

5

6

7

After a snowfall, the east Summer House of the Walled Garden basks in a winter sun. *Photo: Richard Cheek*

J A N U A R Y

8

9

10

11

12

13

14

Delightful lead figures line the colonnade along the dining room roof.
Here the Tambourine Girl plays an eternal rhythm on her instrument. *Photo: Richard Cheek*

J ANUARY

15

16

17

18

19

20

21

The South Façade of Westbury House in winter. The South Allée leading to the house is lined with European lindens. *Photo: Richard Cheek*

JANUARY

22

23

24

25

26

27

28

Detail of the South Allée wrought-iron gates. *Photo: Richard Cheek*

$\mathcal{J}$ A N - $\mathcal{F}$ E B

29

30

31

1

2

3

4

The Boxwood Garden, the West Pond, and Diana's colonnade and reflecting pool are seen
from above by the winged visitors and residents of Old Westbury Gardens. *Photo: Richard Cheek*

FEBRUARY

5

6

7

8

9

10

11

One of the many sundials found at Old Westbury Gardens, this one is on the chimney of the dining room wing of Westbury House. The inscription intended for the space above the cherub was never completed, but it was to have read: *Ora Ne Te Rapiat Hora* (Pray the hour does not snatch you away). *Photo: Richard Cheek*

$\mathcal{F}$ E B R U A R Y

12

13

14

15

16

17

18

One of the large 18th century lead sphinxes (after a design by Robert Adam)
that guard the South Terrace of Westbury House. *Photo: David Enders Tripp*

F E B R U A R Y

19

20

21

22

23

24

25

A spring rain falls gently on the great American beech on the terrace of Westbury House. *Photo: Richard Cheek*

$\mathcal{F}$ E B - $\mathcal{M}$ A R

26

27

28/29

1

2

3

4

In springtime, heavy falls of purple wisteria line the staircase to the South Terrace of Westbury House. *Photo: Richard Cheek*

M A R C H

5

6

7

8

9

10

11

Spring brings a stunning display of grape hyacinths in a field near Westbury House. *Photo: Richard Cheek*

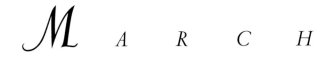

MARCH

12

13

14

15

16

17

18

Colorful Darwin hybrid tulips along the central path of the Walled Garden
are underplanted with pansies – an Old Westbury Gardens trademark. *Photo: Richard Cheek*

MARCH

19

20

21

22

23

24

25

Spring brings multicolored Darwin hybrid tulips to the central pathway of the Walled Garden. *Photo: Richard Cheek*

$\mathcal{M}$ A R - $\mathcal{A}$ P R

26

27

28

29

30

31

1

Eagle Hill, to the west of Westbury House, features a column surmounted by an eagle and, in mid-May, masses of colorful rhododendron. *Photo: Richard Cheek*

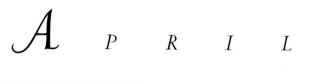

$\mathcal{A}$ P R I L

2

3

4

5

6

7

8

The east pavilion the the Walled Garden is reflected in the Lotus Pool in early spring. *Photo: David Enders Tripp*

9

10

11

12

13

14

15

The central fountain in the lower terrace of the Walled Garden is surrounded by white flowers in tribute to Margarita Grace Phipps, who invariably wore her white pearls. The Italianate garden was created by designer George Crawley and Mrs. Phipps, to whom it is dedicated. *Photo: Richard Cheek*

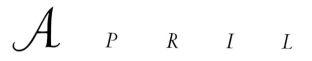

$\mathcal{A}$ P R I L

16

17

18

19

20

21

22

A bright array of foxgloves stands before the west gate of the Walled Garden. *Photo: Richard Cheek*

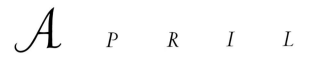

23

24

25

26

27

28

29

The south end of the Walled Garden consists of the dramatic Treillage, an extended trellis that surrounds the Lotus Pool. The walk is lined with lush plantings of cinnamon fern and hosta, while Japanese and Chinese wisteria grow overhead. *Photo: Hugh Palmer*

A P R - *M* A Y

30

1

2

3

4

5

6

A twelve-sided sundial topped by a rampant lion is a focal point of the Rose Garden, designed by George Crawley in parterre fashion. Nearly two hundred hybrid tea roses fill the concentric circles and squares within squares. *Photo: Richard Cheek*

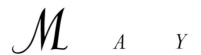

$\mathcal{M}$ A Y

7

8

9

10

11

12

13

The North Façade of Westbury House basks in the late afternoon summer sun. *Photo: Richard Cheek*

M A Y

14

15

16

17

18

19

20

From the wisteria-covered central pavilion of the Treillage in the Walled Garden, the mists of an early summer morning surround the trees while the fountain plays amid the tall Sacred Lotus. *Photo: Richard Cheek*

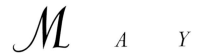

M A Y

21

22

23

24

25

26

27

The wrought-iron gates at the entrance to Old Westbury Gardens were brought from Combermere Abbey to guard this Linden Allée. *Photo: Richard Cheek*

M A Y - J U N E

28

29

30

31

1

2

3

Along the central path of the upper bed of the Walled Garden grow climbing roses supported by posts and chains. Here red and white roses form a romantic heart shape. *Photo: Laura Carpenter*

$\mathcal{J}$ U N E

4

5

6

7

8

9

10

The Thatched Cottage, protected by a silver maple, was a birthday gift to Peggie Phipps as a child. The typical English cottage garden is planted with miniature varieties in keeping with the scale of the house. *Photo: Richard Cheek*

J U N E

11

12

13

14

15

16

17

The north gate of the Walled Garden is a ceremonial arch with wrought-iron gates carrying a floral motif. *Photo: Richard Cheek*

JUNE

18

19

20

21

22

23

24

An overhead view of the Rose Garden shows its parterre design, which resembles an oriental carpet when the roses are in bloom. In the distance through the trees is Westbury House. *Photo: Richard Cheek*

J U N E - J U L Y

25

26

27

28

29

30

1

Another of Old Westbury Gardens' residents, a curious frog admires a water lily on the East Lake. *Photo: Richard Cheek*

JULY

2

3

4

5

6

7

8

An early, misty morning in midsummer finds the Walled Garden a quiet and mysterious place. *Photo: Richard Cheek*

$\mathcal{J}$ U L Y

9

10

11

12

13

14

15

The feathery plumes of Pink Sprite astilbe fill the informal wedge-shaped Pie Garden. *Photo: Richard Cheek*

$\mathcal{J}$ U L Y

16

17

18

19

20

21

22

The Rhododendron Copse, viewed from the balcony of Westbury House, consists primarily of hybrids of Catawba rhododendron, noted for their extreme hardiness. *Photo: Richard Cheek*

$\mathcal{J}$ U L Y

23

24

25

26

27

28

29

Brilliant red and yellow lantana bloom in the Walled Garden. *Photo: Richard Cheek*

$\mathcal{J}$ U L Y - $\mathcal{A}$ U G

30

31

1

2

3

4

5

For decades, the magnificent American beech has shaded the southwestern corner
of the South Terrace of Westbury House from the summer sun. *Photo: Richard Cheek*

$\mathcal{A}$ U G U S T

6

7

8

9

10

11

12

Midsummer plants in the lower terrace of the Walled Garden include achillea, phlox,
Shasta daisies, fuschia, dahlias, asters, hollyhocks, and a variety of annuals. *Photo: Richard Cheek*

AUGUST

13

14

15

16

17

18

19

Pastel lantana in the Walled Garden are enjoyed by butterflies as well as by human visitors. *Photo: Richard Cheek*

$\mathcal{A}$ U G U S T

20

21

22

23

24

25

26

In early summer, Old Westbury Gardens' resident mallards take to the water on the East Lake. *Photo: Richard Cheek*

27

28

29

30

31

1

2

The Eagle Sundial is reflected in the still water of the West Pond. The Swan Ferry is a faithful copy
of the one used by the Phipps children to travel across the pond from bank to bank. *Photo: Richard Cheek*

S E P T E M B E R

3

4

5

6

7

8

9

Ducks enjoy the waters of an Old Westbury Gardens lake. Some enjoy it sufficiently to remain year round. *Photo: Richard Cheek*

10

11

12

13

14

15

16

The South Terrace balustrade of Westbury House provides a view of the broad
grassy South Allée, lined with European lindens. *Photo: Richard Cheek*

S E P T E M B E R

17

18

19

20

21

22

23

Pink ivy-leaf geraniums bloom throughout the summer in the lead urns that line
the balustrade and staircase to the upper terrace of Westbury House. *Photo: David Enders Tripp*

24

25

26

27

28

29

30

The South Façade of Westbury House, which was designed in a Charles II style by George Crawley for John S. and Margarita Grace Phipps. The house was begun in 1904, with work on the gardens starting at nearly the same time. *Photo: David Enders Tripp*

O C T O B E R

1

2

3

4

5

6

7

The west wall of the Walled Garden in summer. *Photo: Richard Cheek*

O C T O B E R

8

9

10

11

12

13

14

The Walled Garden offers a continuous display of colors from spring through fall. Here a dahlia provides a summer splash of crimson. *Photo: Richard Cheek*

O C T O B E R

22

23

24

25

26

27

28

The serene Boxwood Garden, with a marble-trimmed reflecting pool and fountain and a Corinthian colonnade with a
terracotta statue of Diana the Huntress, was created more than two decades after Westbury House was built. Boxwood shrubs,
already a century old, were brought from Virginia to be planted in the garden. *Photo: Richard Cheek*

29

30

31

1

2

3

4

Autumn leaves seen through the delicate wrought-iron canopy of the Temple of Love at the end of the East Lake. *Photo: David Enders Tripp*

N O V E M B E R

5

6

7

8

9

10

11

A stunning display of maples in their autumn dress is reflected in a quiet pond on the estate grounds. *Photo: David Enders Tripp*

12

13

14

15

16

17

18

The reflecting pool in the Boxwood Garden mirrors the colonnade and Diana with her hound. *Photo: Richard Cheek*

$\mathcal{N}$ O V E M B E R

19

20

21

22

23

24

25

The white bark of the gray birch contrasts with the clear blue sky and colorful leaves of autumn. *Photo: David Enders Tripp*

N o v - D e c

26

27

28

29

30

1

2

The west Summer House of the Walled Garden welcomes autumn under the golden leaves of sugar maples. *Photo: Richard Cheek*

$\mathcal{D}$ E C E M B E R

3

4

5

6

7

8

9

Autumn leaves reflected in a pond at Old Westbury Gardens. *Photo: David Enders Tripp*

D ECEMBER

10

11

12

13

14

15

16

Detail of the terracotta Diana in the colonnade of the Boxwood Garden. *Photo: Richard Cheek*

DECEMBER

17

18

19

20

21

22

23

Old Westbury Gardens' famed Rose Garden rests under the snows of winter. *Photo: Richard Cheek*

DECEMBER

24

25

26

27

28

29

30/31

Snow-covered wedding cake topiaries flank the limestone niche in the South Terrace wall of Westbury House. *Photo: Richard Cheek*

NOTES

NOTES